Write Your Faith Autobiography

This Book Belongs to:

Name _____

Phone # _____

Date _____

Write Your Faith Autobiography

For the Spiritual Exercises of St. Ignatius 19th Annotation

Ellen Tomaszewski

Write Your Faith Autobiography
For the Spiritual Exercises of St. Ignatius
19th Annotation

By Ellen Tomaszewski

Also available in Spanish

Copyright © 2023
E. Tomaszewski

ISBN: 978-1-936824-38-0

All rights reserved
http://etcpress.net

etcetera press

Why Write a Faith Autobiography?

For the Spiritual Exercises, you will write the journey of their faith life, an autobiography based on how God has worked through your life. This booklet provides a simple method to do this. You'll answer a daily question that helps you focus on God's presence. There's space to write, so you can put your thoughts down easily.

This process is for you. It will help you see God's actions more clearly.

When finished, you can share this information with your spiritual director who will help you process it.

All information is confidential, of course.

How to Use this Booklet

- Each page includes a prompt for the day.
- Take a few minutes to read then pray about the daily question.
- Write your answer on the lines provided. Try to fill the page.

Once you've completed this booklet, you will have written your faith autobiography and discovered more about God's working in your life.

Week 1

God & My Beginning

Week 1, Day 1   **Date:** _____

To begin, I list my parents' names, birthplaces, birth dates. I will note when and where I was born, and any significant medical details. I try to relate at least one of these facts to God and my spiritual life.

_____

_____

_____

_____

_____

_____

_____

_____

_____

_____

_____

Week 1, Day 2   **Date:** _____

Consider people who have made a difference in my life: siblings and extended family members, friends, or neighbors and note important details about them. How has each one influenced me and my spiritual growth, for good or evil?

_____

_____

_____

_____

_____

_____

_____

_____

_____

_____

_____

_____

_____

Week 1, Day 3   **Date:** _____

I'll list places I've lived. I pray about each one, and consider how these places impacted my impression of life, of love, of God, and of others.

_____

_____

_____

_____

_____

_____

_____

_____

_____

_____

_____

_____

_____

Week 1, Day 4 Date: _____

I choose one of the places I've lived (from yesterday) and pray about it today. How was it important to my spiritual growth?

_____

_____

_____

_____

_____

_____

_____

_____

_____

_____

_____

_____

_____

Week 1 Day 5 Date: _____

I list (6 or so) positive qualities or characteristics that I have. *(For example, maybe I'm quiet or outgoing, thorough, sensitive, or truthful. Do I have lots of energy and accomplish a great deal? Am I'm healthy, good at singing, honest, etc.?)* Next to each trait, I'll list why I consider this characteristic to be positive, and what I think God has to do with it.

_____

_____

_____

_____

_____

_____

_____

_____

_____

_____

_____

_____

Week 1, Day 6 Date: _____

Today I think and pray about the circumstances I've contemplated up to now– family, society, religious upbringing, etc. How have they influenced my view of God?

_____
_____
_____
_____
_____
_____
_____
_____
_____
_____
_____

Week 1, Day 7   **Date:** _____

I take several minutes to think back on the week. What rises to the top of mind for me, and what seems important to my faith life?

_____

_____

_____

_____

_____

_____

_____

_____

_____

_____

_____

_____

Week 2

Who Am I According To Me, and According To God?

Week 2, Day 1   **Date:** _____

What is my nationality and religious heritage? How have my sex, race, ethnicity, and physical build molded who I am?

_____

_____

_____

_____

_____

_____

_____

_____

_____

_____

_____

_____

Week 2, Day 2   Date: _____

Make a list of 4 or 5 characteristics of myself that I would rather not have. (Too tall or short, lose my temper too quickly, not careful enough, etc.) Why don't I like these traits?

_____

_____

_____

_____

_____

_____

_____

_____

_____

_____

_____

Week 2, Day 3   **Date:** _____

Now that I've considered my good and bad traits, background, and influences, where do I see God in those things, or do I? Who is God for me, considering all that?

_____

_____

_____

_____

_____

_____

_____

_____

_____

_____

_____

_____

_____

Week 2, Day 4   **Date:** _____

What great sorrow, tragedy, or suffering have I experienced and in what ways have any of those been important in my faith journey?

_____

_____

_____

_____

_____

_____

_____

_____

_____

_____

_____

Week 2, Day 5 **Date:** _____

What are some of the things that cause me to feel separate from God? Why? Do my negative traits impact this? How?

Week 2, Day 6   **Date:** _____

What are some of the things that cause me to feel connected to God? Why? How does this connection affect me and my prayer life?

_____

_____

_____

_____

_____

_____

_____

_____

_____

_____

_____

Week 2, Day 7   **Date:** _____

Look over your week. What stands out for me? I ask God to help me explore that more deeply today.

_____

_____

_____

_____

_____

_____

_____

_____

_____

_____

_____

_____

Week 3

How Do God & I Relate to One Another?

Week 3, Day 1   **Date:**_____

How does separation from God in the areas prayed about last week affect my spiritual life, my well-being, my prayer?

_____

_____

_____

_____

_____

_____

_____

_____

_____

_____

_____

Week 3, Day 2 **Date:** _____

Are there areas that I think God wants to make use of me for others? What are they? How do I feel about this?

Week 3, Day 3 **Date:** _____

Here, I'll list some of the choices I've made during my faith journey. Looking back, I notice some that were helpful, and some that were not. Some I am glad I made, some I regret. What does God say about them?

_____

_____

_____

_____

_____

_____

_____

_____

_____

_____

_____

_____

Week 3, Day 4   **Date:** _____

Here, I choose one life experience that transformed me in some way. This might be a great joy or a time of conversion. What happened to my prayer life because of that experience?

_____

_____

_____

_____

_____

_____

_____

_____

_____

_____

_____

_____

Week 3, Day 5   **Date:** _____

Here I'll discuss what I did in the past when I felt dryness in prayer.

_____

_____

_____

_____

_____

_____

_____

_____

_____

_____

_____

_____

Week 3, Day 6   **Date:** _____

Where do I find God in my daily life outside of prayer? Explain in detail.

_____

_____

_____

_____

_____

_____

_____

_____

_____

_____

_____

Week 3, Day 7   **Date:** _____

I review what I wrote during this week about my choices and gifts.

Week 4

Where is God in My Future?

Week 4, Day 1   **Date:** _____

What trends do I see in my faith journey? For instance, do I start enthused but my interest wanes over time? Do I start slowly and build interest? In general, right now, is my journey rocky or smooth, hard or easy? Explain.

_____

_____

_____

_____

_____

_____

_____

_____

_____

_____

_____

_____

Week 4, Day 2 Date: _____

I re-read what I wrote during Week 3. Are there areas in me that I feel God wants to love, but I won't let Him in? What are they and why do I think this?

Week 4, Day 3   **Date:** _____

What in me do I think God wants to change? How do I feel about this?

_____

_____

_____

_____

_____

_____

_____

_____

_____

_____

_____

Week 4, Day 4   **Date:** _____

Where do I feel most known or understood by God? Why?

Week 4, Day 5   **Date:** _____

Are there any parts of my life that I have a hard time imagining God accepting me or understanding me as I am? Why?

_____
_____
_____
_____
_____
_____
_____
_____
_____
_____
_____
_____

Week 4, Day 6   **Date:** _____

In general, how is my prayer life? What aspects of prayer do I like, and what aspects do I think need to be improved upon?

_____

_____

_____

_____

_____

_____

_____

_____

_____

_____

_____

Week 4, Day 7 Date_____

In summary, the following describes some of the highlights that I discovered about myself as I prayed through my life and history:

_____
_____
_____
_____
_____
_____
_____
_____
_____
_____
_____
_____
_____

Dear Participant,

Thank-you for writing your faith autobiography. We hope the process has enriched you and helped clarify and expand your understanding of God's deep connection to you throughout your whole life.

We love you.

Your Retreat Team

www.ingramcontent.com/pod-product-compliance
Lightning Source LLC
LaVergne TN
LVHW051206080426
835508LV00021B/2845